582
Wi   Withner
A Book of Orchids

DATE DUE

OCT 27 1989			
MAR 1 9 1997			
MAR 2 4 1999			
FEB 2 2 2006			

A BOOK OF
ORCHIDS

BY
DR. CARL WITHNER
ILLUSTRATIONS BY JUAN LUIS G. VELA

William Morrow and Company, Inc.
New York

A QUARTO BOOK

Library of Congress Catalog Card Number: 84-61803

ISBN 0-688-04103-5

A BOOK OF ORCHIDS
was produced and prepared by
Quarto Marketing Ltd.
15 West 26th Street,
New York, N.Y. 10010

Editor: Mary Forsell
Art Director/Designer: Richard Boddy

Typeset by BPE Graphics, Inc.
Color separations by
Hong Kong Scanner Craft Company Ltd.
Printed and bound in Hong Kong by
Leefung-Asco Printers Ltd.

First Edition

1 2 3 4 5 6 7 8 9 10

CONTENTS

Dedicated to all those orchid growers
who started out with only *one* plant!

A GRATEFUL THANK-YOU TO Dorothy Harrison
of Planting Fields Arboretum who offered her expert
knowledge. Additional thank-yous go to Keith Lloyd
of the New York Botanical Garden and to Heidi Friedman
of the New York Horticultural Society.

INTRODUCTION

Orchids are among the most exciting plant families—to find in the wild, to grow, to study, to show or judge, or just to look at. Their colors, varieties, and forms never cease to amaze! There are more than 25,000 species and more than 75,000 cultivated hybrids. It takes a while to know them, but this little book may give an idea of their special appeal, from the classic *Laeliocattleya* corsage orchid to the exotic *Paphiopedilum*.

Orchids are highly evolved botanically and show their specializations in a variety of ways: some externally, in the ways the flowers are formed and adapted to specific insects for pollination; others internally, in terms of their biochemical processes. We shall explore some of these for your pleasure and information, and you can appreciate their exotic beauty at the same time.

Orchids are found throughout the world in all but the Arctic and Antarctic circles. The orchids native to the northern temperate zones are small terrestrial plants that often grow in bogs or sometimes in woodland habitats. In the tropics, however, most orchids are epiphytes, that is, they grow perched upon the branches and trunks of trees, habitats that serve to raise them up off the forest floor and into the sunlight. They do not parasitize the trees, but only sit upon them with the other epiphytes: air plants, mosses, ferns, and a variety of other species. When transplanted to the greenhouse and conditions for cultivation, they must be grown in porous bark mixtures to duplicate their airy home perches.

Soil is much too compact for growing any but the orchids that originally came from it. Most ground-growing orchids transplant badly; therefore they must be conserved in their natural locations. Most naturalists and collectors keep such locations secret, since many terrestrial orchid species are rare. Today the International Endangered Species Convention protects all orchids when it comes to trade, but little protects them from the deforestation processes that result from population pressures, particularly in the tropics.

Now, just what is an orchid? The botanical explanation is primarily concerned with the structure of the flowers. Regardless of their size or particular form, all orchids share certain components. The sepals are three outer parts that protect the bud. When open, they color-up like petals. Inside the sepals are the three petals. The lip, or labellum, is distinctly different from the other two petals. The lip is a result of the adaptation of the flower to a specific type of pollinator and is, in a sense, a "landing field" to accommodate the visitor. Finally, the stamens and carpels are fused together into a single structure called the column. The lip and column are so positioned that the pollinator, visiting the flower for the nectar, fragrant oils, or other food, contacts the pollen in the visit and carries it on to the next flower, thereby assuring cross-pollination.

Orchids have a unique vegetative form. Their stems, when swollen with storage tissue for water and food, are called pseudobulbs (not true bulbs). A spongy white layer over the roots, called the velamen, soaks up any water and nutrients available and passes them on to these storage areas.

The habitats of many orchids are surprising as well. They are able to live in their tree-top environments with occasional rain or just night dews to supply their liquid requirements. Some orchids, unbelievably, live on cacti in desert areas where there is no significant rainfall and only nightly condensation of moisture when the temperature drops.

The seeds of orchids are also unusual. They are tiny, almost dust-sized; there may be as many as 3 million in a single seed capsule, which can take several months to ripen. The orchid seed embryo is immature compared to more conventional seeds and has little stored food. In nature, the germinating orchid seed must set up housekeeping with a beneficial fungus, producing a delicate mycorrhizal association. The fungus supplies food for growth until the leaves develop and the plant becomes independent. In the laboratory, it is possible to duplicate the fungal effects with sugars, minerals, and even vitamins and hormones. Thousands of seedlings may thus be grown artifically, in comparison to the few that survive and grow in nature. There is no longer a dependence upon the critical mycorrhizal stage, and after their first one or two years in the cultures they are large enough to be ready for potting out and growing on to flowering. These steps, which can't be rushed, help explain the time, expense, and care required in raising orchids in cultivation. The process from seed to flower may require anywhere from three to seven or ten years.

Orchid cultivation began in the Orient, and Confucius (551–479 B.C.) was among the first orchid fanciers. His phrase, the "king of the fragrant plants," epitomizes the qualities considered desirable in orchids today—graceful leaves, perfumed smell, a certain elegance of habit. Confucius was referring to Chinese *Cymbidiums*, which are still favorites in the Orient.

The Greeks collected wild orchids for their medicinal properties according to what became the Doctrine of Signatures, the belief that plants showed by their structures how they could be used to treat various diseases. The Mediterranean terrestrial orchids had underground tubers in pairs, so they were presumed to be good for sexual difficulties. In fact, the word "orchid" comes from the Greek *orchis*, meaning testis. In his pharmacopoeia, the famous and influential physician Dioscorides told how the tubers could be used to beget either male or female children, or if used unwisely, to "stirreth up the lust." One can only imagine how many hundreds of orchids were destroyed over the centuries by followers of Dioscorides' advice. Medieval herbalists were still repeating Dioscorides' recipes in their "herbals," which were illustrated treatises on plants. The herbalists attempted to describe and illustrate all known plants, including orchids, but the Greeks' superstitions still prevailed.

The next significant developments in orchid history occurred in 1768, when botanists at Kew Gardens began cultivating orchids. Meanwhile, Europeans traveling abroad brought back odd orchid plants from Asia to grow in their overheated greenhouses called "stoves." The tough pseudobulbous plants were able to survive those voyages, which took two or three months or more. The actual "first" was likely a plant of the genus *Bletia*, which was sent from the Bahamas to the famous horticulturist Peter Collinson in 1731. Starting out in the form of a dried herbarium specimen, it proceeded to grow and flower the following year.

Since that time, orchids have continued to grow in numbers, popularity, and worldwide availability. In these pages, many genera of the Orchidaceae are presented. A variety of beautiful species within these genera are described, and a number of hybrids appear as well. They are presented alphabetically according to common name. Hybrid names serve as common names, followed by the genus and a selection name, which indicates parentage. The date of hybridization is also included, when known. Ordinarily, the genus name would precede the hybrid common name (e.g. *Phalaenopsis* Alfonso Ibarra), but the hybrids names have been shortened here for clarity. Only a few species of orchids have informal common names, and these vary both regionally and internationally. For those species orchids in this book that do not have common names, we've taken the liberty of either translating their Greek- or Latin-based names, or assigning a name based on the flower's history. Their scientific names follow. If you wish to obtain species plants, rely on their scientific names and you'll be speaking the universal botanical language.

Growing orchids is no longer a rich person's hobby. You don't need greenhouses to grow these stunning flowers. There are many that grow well on windowsills or under lights, and the plants are easily available for reasonable sums. Although some selected orchids may be very expensive, the newer techniques of cloning, plus the more usual production of orchids from seeds, help keep costs down.

If you've not grown orchids before, this little book may encourage you to join the thousands who already enjoy their fascinating beauty. But there's a real caveat here—if you have one orchid plant, you will want more! This volume shows you why.

ALFONSO IBARRA

PHALAENOPSIS
Hugo Freed x P.J. Beard

~

There are many Moth Orchids derived from species other than the familiar white forms. They may be pink, brown, yellow, or even pale green, and may be barred, spotted, or striped in darker colors. The lips also may be a contrasting color. Stripes first appeared accidentally in some hybrids while breeders were attempting to achieve all-pink flowers, but now they are popular in themselves. Since *Phalaenopsis* are quickly grown from seed, they are more reasonably priced than other types of orchids, and many hobbyists grow them exclusively. They must, however, be provided with humid, warm conditions typical of equatorial Asia. After the initial flowering the flower stalks will send out secondary and even tertiary branches, so the plants continue to flower over many months. Most "phals" are sensitive to pollution, which may cause the buds and flowers to wilt in only a few hours. They require clean air for successful cultivation.

Amboina moth orchid

Phalaenopsis
P. amboinensis

~

The Moth Orchids may be roughly divided into three color classes today—the whites, the pinks, and spotted or novelty crosses, which range in color from cream to yellow to various "sunset" shades. The spottings of the novelty types, especially the yellow forms, may often be traced back to this *Phalaenopsis* and similar species that come from the Moluccas in Indonesia. It is easy to cultivate under lights, as are all *Phalaenopsis* plants. Many people choose to grow these because they develop more quickly from seed to flowering than other kinds of orchids and, accordingly, are cheaper to buy. The same flower spike may continue branching and blooming over a period of two or three years. Everyone looks for an ever-blooming orchid, and this type most nearly fills the bill.

AMETHYST-LIPPED

CATTLEYA

CATTLEYA
C. amethystoglossa

~

Of the Brazilian bifoliate *Cattleyas,* this species is one of the most spectacularly beautiful. A well-grown specimen is stately and may reach a height of 3 to 4 feet, producing more than twenty 3- to 4-inch flowers. They may vary from pale ivory to blush pink and are spotted with the deep purple color that gives it its name. The lip also is the color of amethyst. The plant was first cultivated in Europe around 1850, when the first sample plants were sent from Brazil to Germany.

BEAUTIFUL ONCIDIUM

ONCIDIUM
O. pulchellum

~

This spritely pink *Oncidium* is endemic to Jamaica and is one of about thirty-five species found on the Caribbean islands. They are generally termed equitant *Oncidiums*, as the leaves are flattened and produced in the form of a fan. The disturbance of natural habitats on the islands for so many years has led to the formation of many natural hybrids. Many others have been produced in cultivation. They come in a rainbow of colors and patterns, and *O. pulchellum* has often been used as a major parent because of its dark colors and comparatively large flower size.

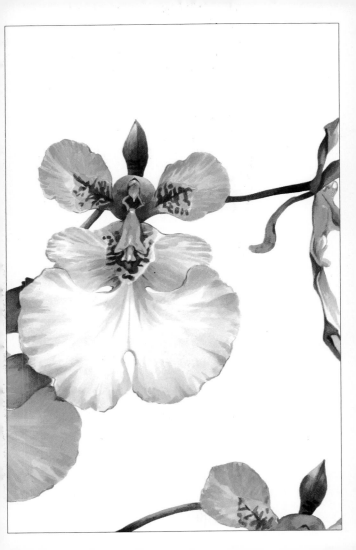

BOCA DEL DRAGON

ENCYCLIA

E. cordigera var. *alba*

~

This orchid was known for many years as the species *atropurpurea*, meaning a dark purple color, and then an older valid name was discovered referring to the heart-shaped lip. By now most people have changed the labels on their plants, but the other name is still used by some. It is a popular species and is found from Venezuela northward into Guatemala and Mexico. In Guatemala it is called *Boca del Dragon*. The sepals typically curl forward at their tips, a quality passed on to hybrids, and the color can vary from greenish with a maroon wash to dark rosy purple. The typical form has a white lip with a few purple lines at the base, but the lip on the variety *roseum* is purple overall. It has been cultivated in England since 1836, introduced by a Mr. Horsfall of Liverpool, an early orchid fancier.

BOSCHII

~

This striking hybrid *Vanda* is a primary cross between two species, one from the Philippines, *V. luzonica,* and the other from Java, *V. tricolor.* It was registered as Boschii by the Munich Botanical Garden in 1928, when Latinized flower names were still popular. This is no longer possible by our present international rules for naming new hybrids, a procedure established to avoid confusion with botanical scientific names for plants. Both parents are reflected in the white flowers with magenta purple spottings, and they are extremely fragrant. The fully grown plant may have several stems, each of which can grow to about 3 or 4 feet, producing the many-flowered sprays. The plants have heavy, long roots that would attach the plants to trees if they were growing in nature. In cultivation they just hang in the air around the base of the plant.

BOUTON D'OR

BRASSOLAELIOCATTLEYA

Cattleya Wolteriana x *Blc.* Buttercup, 1968

～

These beautiful golden flowers result from several generations of breeding, and the cross has won many awards. It is noted for its good shape, long-lasting quality, and uniform color. The full wide lip comes from the *Brassavola* parentage, the shape and color from its *Cattleya* background, and its vigor from the *Laelia.* It is thus a multigenerational trigeneric hybrid and one of the best concolor yellow hybrids grown today.

BUTTERFLY ONCIDIUM

ONCIDIUM
O. papilio

~

Oncidium is a genus with a great variety of more than three hundred species in the New World. None is so unique or easily recognized as the group that includes the three Butterfly Orchids. The lateral petals and dorsal sepal look like the giant antennae of an exotic creature as the flower nods from its perch on the end of a long, curving stalk. The lateral sepals are colored like the lip. Although only a single flower blooms at a time, the stalk can continue producing flowers steadily for two or three years. The leaves are also attractive, being olive-green strongly mottled in red. This species is found in Venezuela and Trinidad and has also been raised from seed in cultivation. It has been used as a parent in hybrids, but most prefer it just as a species. *Papilio* is the genus of the swallowtail butterfly, after which the orchid was apparently named when it was introduced in England in 1824.

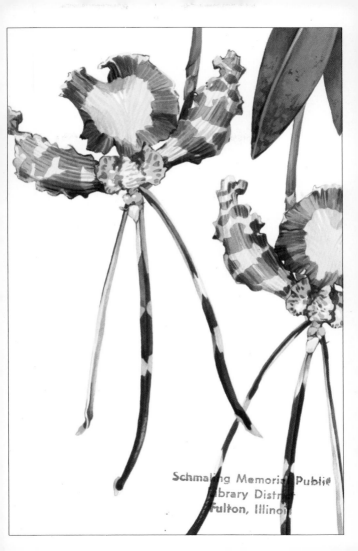

CALIFORNIA
'CASCADE'

CYMBIDIUM
Blue Smoke x Alexanderi, 1955

~

Cymbidiums are popular winter flowers, cheaper to buy and easier to produce in quantity for the market than *Cattleyas*. They are descended from Indian species found in Darjeeling and Bengal and are excellent subjects for the cool greenhouse, though standard *Cymbidiums* are large plants to accommodate. Ideal for southern California, they may be grown in beds of compost in a protected garden from about San Francisco south. A full-grown plant may produce several sprays of fifteen to twenty flowers each, and they may last for a month or more in perfect condition. They are grown by the thousands on Long Island in New York and in Holland. New Zealand and Australia also produce them "down under," with the reverse of our seasons, to make them available to florists the year round.

CANTATA

CYMBIDIUM
Early Bird x Sicily, 1966

~

This *Cymbidium* is one of the hybridizers' attempts
to produce a plant that will flower in the fall instead
of the winter, when most *Cymbidiums* are in bloom.
Cymbidiums come in a variety of colors, mostly
pastel pinks, creams, greens, and whites, but
breeders are trying to produce reds and other more
vibrant tones as well. Since there is a whole range of
miniature *Cymbidium* species available, the new
hybrids, such as this one, are also smaller in size. As
a result, four to six plants can be grown in the same
space as one large, standard type. The Chinese and
Japanese have grown the miniature types for
hundreds of years.

Cinnabar laelia

Laelia

L. cinnabarina

~

This Brazilian *Laelia*, really more orange than the reddish tint of cinnabar, is, nevertheless, brilliant and starry and a fine orchid. It is used much in modern hybrids and is dominant in transmitting its color and shape, right down to the crimped and frilled lip. Orange is still a color hard to find in the larger-flowered *Cattleya*-type hybrids, and it requires several generations of breeding to obtain the combination of size and color. This is one of a number of so-called Rock Laelias—they grow on the rocks in certain mountain areas of central Brazil, exposed to full sun with their roots in cracks and crevices, and without water during the dry season. They produce tough plants with stiff leathery leaves and in cultivation grow well in pumice or volcanic rock mixtures.

CRESCENT BEACH

ASCOCENDA

Vanda Ohuohu x *Ascda.* Red Gem, 1976

~

The *Ascocentrums,* from which hybrids such as this one have been bred, are bright orange, yellow, pink, or purple and produce several short sprays of flowers simultaneously. They combine readily with the larger *Vandas* to make medium-sized plants with warm vibrant colors. The hybrids are extremely popular these days, especially in warm areas, where they can be grown out-of-doors. They stand up to the sun and produce a rainbow of colors. Popular in Hawaii, Singapore, Thailand, Florida, and California, the plants are not strictly seasonal and may flower at various times during the year. When *Ascocentrums* are spotted or marked, these traits come from the *Vanda* side of the family. The original parents come from India and Thailand.

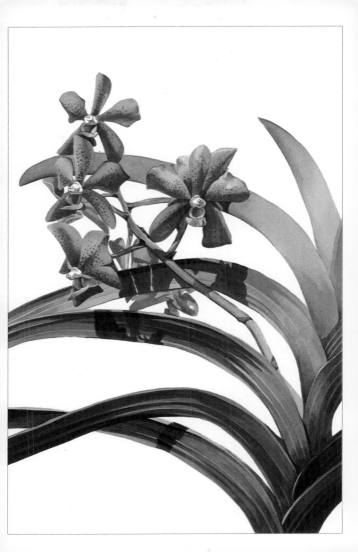

CULMINANT
'LA TUILERIE'

LAELIOCATTLEYA

Ile de France x Gaillard, 1957

~

Modern hybrids of *Laeliocattleya* have more intense color as a result of breeding and selection, and more vigor and floriferousness than the parental species could show. This hybrid represents seven generations of hybridizing, approximately fifty years, to get its dark color, full shape, and fine lip, and it has won awards for its French originators, the company of Vacherot & Lecoufle. The flowers are sweetly fragrant on the plant, but as with other orchids they lose their perfume once cut, thus giving the impression that orchids lack fragrance. Many, if not most orchids do have it!

DIGBY'S
RHYNCHOLAELIA

RHYNCHOLAELIA
R. (Brassavola) digbyana

~

This orchid is famous for its large green flowers with
remarkably fringed lips and a strong nighttime
fragrance. On some flowers the petals are fringed too.
This species has been much used in modern
Cattleya hybrids to produce large, frilled lip petals,
or to produce unusual green flowers. The plants
grow naturally on scrubby trees, fully exposed to the
tropical sun and with their roots running for several
feet along the branches. They are found in Yucatán
and farther south in sea-level habitats with sufficient
light and heat.

DORIS HUNTER

PAPHIOPEDILUM
Doris Stanton x Mildred Hunter, 1949

~

Spotted green and brown lady's slippers are not liked by all orchid growers, some of whom call them "toads." Such epithets hardly reflect their strange beauty. They are descended from several different species of Indian lady's slippers, the most dominant of which is *Paphiopedilum insigne,* which contributes the spotted pattern to the hybrids. The flowers often appear waxed or varnished, but the high gloss is natural and enhances their beauty. They come from cliffs and crevices in mountain forest areas, so require cool conditions for cultivation. They bloom from late fall into winter and have been grown for years as ideal houseplants on a shady, cool windowsill.

DWARF FIRE ORCHID

RENANTHERA
R. monachica

～

Renanthera is a tropical Asiatic genus with usually large and robust plants that may climb many feet into trees, reaching for the full tropical sun for flowering. But this species from Luzon in the Philippines is the baby of the genus, growing only 1 or 2 feet in height. That, naturally, makes it more popular than its 10-foot relatives for greenhouse culture. The Fire Orchids flower in a spray. The flowers are unusual in that the sepals are larger than the petals and the lip is the smallest part of all—just the reverse of the normal arrangement of an orchid flower. Also, the lateral sepals are nearly parallel. All the flowers of this group are bright red or orange with spottings of dark red, so they always make an intense color mark wherever they grow, usually the hot, humid areas near the Equator. These are conditions hard to provide in the greenhouse, so they are best cultivated out-of-doors.

FLOWER OF
SAN SEBASTIAN

CATTLEYA

C. skinneri var. *alba*

❧

The national flower of Costa Rica, the Flower of San Sebastian is called *guaria morada* in Spanish and has appeared on stamps and money, as collectors well know. This is a rare white form of a usually purple species and has been found only a very few times in nature, three or four perhaps. Now more are being produced in cultivation by self-pollinating the white flowers for seed. This species is often used for producing spring-flowering hybrids with clusters of flowers on multiple growths. A specimen plant after ten years may be a meter across with 35 to 40 flower heads and 300 to 400 blooms—a magnificent sight.

GENE PAGE FLEET

PAPHIOPEDILUM
Diversion x Walter Moore, 1970

~

This lady's slipper is a hybrid characterized by the cool-growing Indian species in its background. The dorsal sepal of the flower is particularly outstanding with its wide, flat shape and distinct veining. The division of color in the petals is typical, with the lower halves a paler color than the upper. The boss-like shield-shaped structure in the center is the modified third stamen of the flower, the other two remaining functional behind it. No one quite understands its function, but it must aid in attracting pollinator bees. In each species this stamenode has a distinctive shape, and the hybrid is intermediate between them. The pouch-like lip, or slipper, has in-turned upper margins to temporarily hold the bee and force it to brush against the pollen, which sticks to its back as it emerges, to be carried on to another flower.

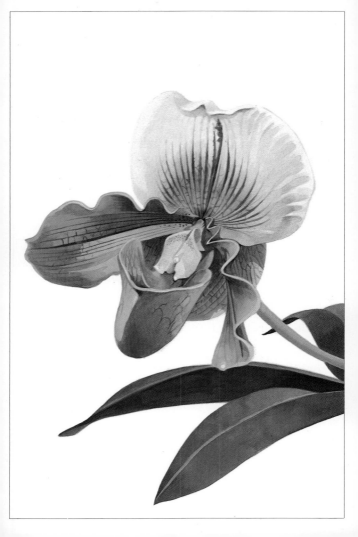

GOLDEN GIFT

PHALAENOPSIS
Golden Buddha x Deventeriana, 1982

~

Hybridizers have been trying to produce a yellow
Phalaenopsis, especially one without spots, for a
long time; but since the two characteristics are
seemingly inherited together, crosses like this one
are the usual result. They are attractive in their own
right, but there are never more than two or three
flowers in bloom at the same time, and they are
usually smaller in size than those of the parent
plants. If these flowers are pollinated to make seed,
the petals turn green, become more fleshy, and
remain on the fruit helping to produce food for the
developing seed. So many crosses were being
registered with the Royal Horticultural Society that
they will accept no more names starting with
"Golden." No one seems interested in emphasizing
the spots!

GRAND LAELIA

LAELIA

L. grandis

❧

Of the various large-flowered *Laelia* species from Brazil, only this one is what the old books used to call nankeen-yellow, the color of a once common cloth made of natural silk. The twisted and quilled petals are typical, as is the white lip veined in rose-purple. This *Laelia* grows in the hot humid areas in Bahia, Brazil, but is rare now in nature. It was first cultivated in 1849 in Paris. Since the shape of the petals is strongly inherited, it is not a species much desired for hybridizing, as flat, fully rounded flowers are the only kind that seem to receive awards.

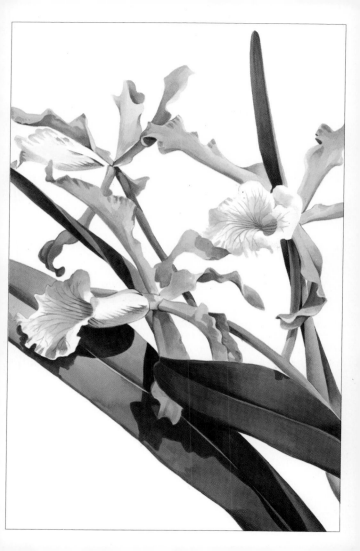

GRAPE-COLORED
VANDA HYBRID

<small>VANDA</small>

Mamo Beauty x Rothschildiana
unregistered

～

This is a hybrid *Vanda*, a cross between a bronzy
red-veined one and a blue one. The results, as you
see, are a dark violet-purple with a deep
grape-colored lip. These kinds of blued dark colors
are much in demand by orchid growers at present
and have necessitated that a new color class be
designated in shows in order to judge them properly
with their peers. Blue colors are still among the
rarest in orchids, as in other flowers, and so are at a
premium. Also, this is a semi-terete *Vanda*, meaning
the leaves are fleshier than usual and do not widen
or flatten out. The plants of most *Vandas* like
equatorial heat and humidity for growth, so they do
well in Singapore, Thailand, and Hawaii, or in a
warm, bright greenhouse.

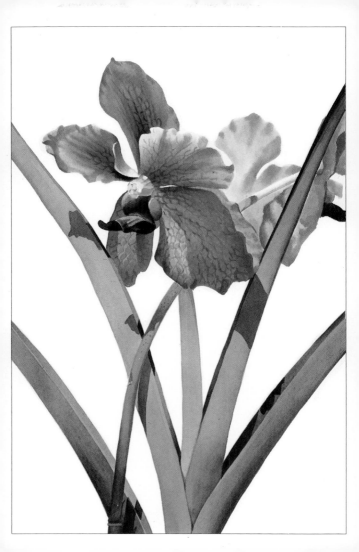

HALAWA BEAUTY

DENDROBIUM
Calvin Morioka x Dora Zane, 1968

~

This hybrid was registered by Tanimoto from Hawaii
in 1968. It is a so-called intersectional dendrobe
hybrid that combines rather distantly related parents
in a new combination. The long sprays are produced
at the top of thick stems. These orchids generally
like heat and humidity, so they do well under
Hawaiian conditions out-of-doors as borders or in
patio containers, where they can reach amazing size.
The flowers last for several weeks, even when cut,
and are readily sold by florists for bouquets and
arrangements. The violet-purple color is a little
unusual, as it is more ordinarily plain purple or
green and brown in this category of orchids.

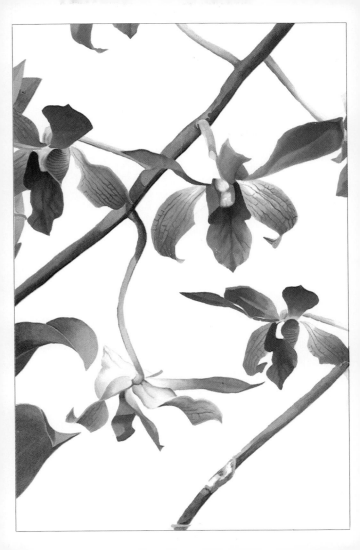

HARRY DUNN

SCHOMBOCATTLEYA

Cattleya Rowena Prowe x *Schomburgkia
lueddemanniana,* 1955

～

Schomburgkia is a genus of large-growing plants
with long wandlike stalks bearing terminal tufts of
flowers. The blooms are usually crisped and floppy.
These plants enjoy heat and sun, growing at sea
level in Central America and northern South
America, and are as tough as they come. By crossing
with *Cattleya,* the plant size is brought down to a
reasonable stature and the flowers are improved in
color and shape. They still tolerate rough growing
conditions, so make good candidates for outdoor
culture in Florida and in tropical gardens.

HAYNALD'S

PAPHIOPEDILUM

PAPHIOPEDILUM
P. haynaldianum

~

Haynald's "paph" belongs to a small group of lady's slippers that regularly produce two to six large spreading flowers on a long stalk, though they may not all be open together. This species was first discovered by Gustav Wallis in 1870 and was introduced by Veitch in England for cultivation in 1873. It came from San Isidro, near Manila, in the Philippines and is named after Cardinal Haynald, an archbishop of Hungary who also was a botanist. The plants can grow into fine specimens bearing numerous flowers on several stems, and they flower from January through March.

IMPERIAL GARDEN

WILSONARA

Odontioda Trixette x *Odontocidium* Tiger Butter, 1978

The large-flowered *Odontoglossum* orchids grow mostly in the cool Andes from Colombia to Peru and are often bred with warmer-growing *Oncidiums* to make the plants more tolerant of temperate climates. This *Wilsonara* is such a result and represents several generations of fine achievement and three genera of orchids. These crosses often produce brown and yellow flowers from the *Oncidium* side of the family, and they inherit what is called the calico patterning from the *Odontoglossum* side. Fifteen or twenty flowers or more are carried on long, branched sprays. The genus is named after Guerney Wilson, an English orchid grower and fancier who was also a writer and editor of orchid journals.

JEWEL BOX

SOPHROLAELIOCATTLEYA
Cattleya aurantiaca x *Slc.* Anzac, 1962

~

This is one of our most popular red hybrids today and has both orange and yellow flowers in its lineage. The red, however, comes from the miniature species of *Sophronitis coccinea* from Brazil, as does its smaller-than-usual plant size and its habit of producing multiple growths. Until recently good red, full, flat flowers have been difficult to achieve, but Californian and Japanese orchid breeders have made the breakthroughs by using a red hybrid that was created in England in 1922, *Sophrolaeliocattleya* Anzac by name. Red hybrids have always been in great demand and have been expensive and hard to get, but now several new ones have been produced. Two especially fine forms of Jewel Box, 'Scheherazade' and 'Dark Waters,' have been propagated by cloning (meristemming) techniques, thus making the plants generally available at reasonable prices.

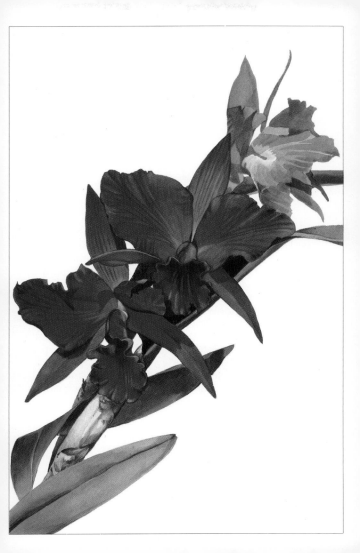

LADY OF THE NIGHT

BRASSAVOLA

B. nodosa

～

The Lady of the Night orchid is fragrant only after dark and can perfume a whole room. Pollinated by night-flying moths, this particular species is found in Central and South America. The fragrance disappears if the plant is exposed to light. A good species for beginners to grow, it is tolerant of light and heat and in nature may even be found growing near the sea on rocks that get salt spray. One never tires of its sturdy floriferous qualities, so it is found in nearly all collections today. It is much used as a parent to make colorful starry-flowered hybrids and is dominant as far as flower shape is concerned.

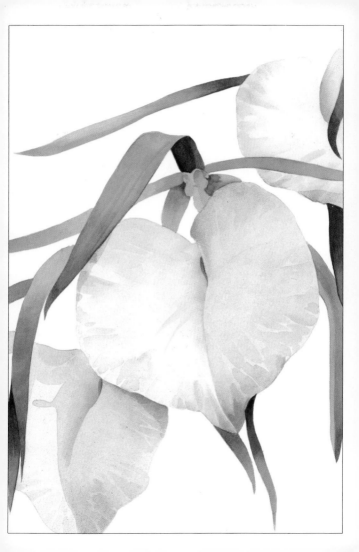

LAELIOCATTLEYA
CORSAGE ORCHID

LAELIOCATTLEYA
Laelia x *Cattleya*

~

Laeliocattleyas, crosses between *Laelia* and
Cattleya, typify the quintessential orchid. This is the
classic orchid for corsages, and is all too often worn
upside down. As a result of breeding and selection,
modern hybrids have more intense color, and more
vigor and floriferousness than the parental species
could show. This hybrid represents generations of
hybridizing to get its unusual color, full shape, and
fine lip.

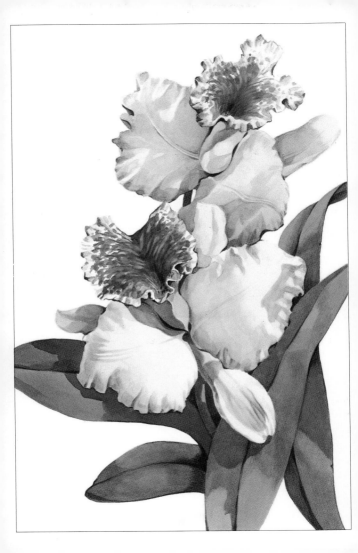

LITTLE MISS MUFFET

CATTLEYA

C. guttata x Prospector, 1974

〜

Pink is a difficult color to achieve in *Cattleya* orchids
as it is usually tinged with lavender or purple.
Surprisingly, this combination worked out well for
the hybridizer in that the color is clear, and yet one
of its parents is a green-bronze color with spottings
of magenta. This hybrid has bifoliate *Cattleya*
characteristics in the tall stems with double leaves,
and a name to match the pert flowers. This type of
Cattleya was once known as a "cocktail" orchid,
because the medium-sized flowers were good for
afternoon corsage wear, but, need I say, little heed is
paid to such amenities any more.

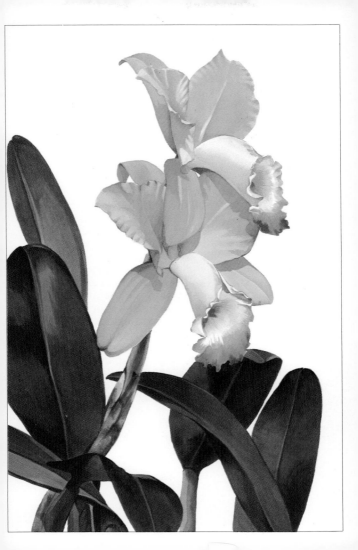

LUM SUM

VANDA HYBRID
parentage unknown

~

For many years the best *Vandas* were bred in Hawaii, and many still are, but there are even more now in Thailand and Singapore—enough for a world supply. The Japanese are also much interested in them and nursery beds are often planted with so many small seedlings that they look like beds of grass. *Vandas* vary a great deal in shape and color according to their backgrounds, some being flat and round, others more starry, and the markings can be either veined or spotted as in this example. The plants are usually grown in hanging baskets so their large aerial roots can hang in the air. They will not stay in pots, much to the frustration of beginning growers; the *Vandas* are epiphytes par excellence. It is striking to see a hedge of these plants along a driveway or back fence in Hawaii. Because of the long narrow leaves, this type of *Vanda* is called a strap-leaf to distinguish it from other types. The lips of the flowers all have short nectar spurs that are seen clearly as the bud develops.

MALONES
'FANTASY'

DENDROBIUM
Akatuki x Glorious Rainbow, 1973

~

This hybrid dendrobe is descended mainly from *Dendrobium nobile,* a popular orchid species from India that is used extensively for breeding because of its easy culture and floriferous habits. Various chromosome races of these plants have been found, and now the pentaploid hybrids, such as this one produced by the Yamamoto family, are being grown commercially in Japan and Hawaii for their large flowers which come in a kaleidoscope of colors. They are sold as elegant potted plants for midwinter holiday occasions. The flowers will last for six weeks, and a well-grown specimen may have forty to fifty blooms completely covering the stems from top to bottom—very showy indeed! These make good houseplants in cool, sunny windows and can go on from year to year, so enjoyment of their perfection is not limited to greenhouse growers. The 'Fantasy' clone of the hybrid was singled out for a special name because of its fine color and shape.

MAUDIAE

PAPHIOPEDILUM
P. callosum x *P. lawrenceanum*, 1900

~

From the mottled-leaved warm-growing lady's slippers of Thailand and other parts of southern Asia, many hybrids have been produced in cultivation. Maudiae is the hybrid of two albino parents that lack the normal red and brown pigmentation that usually colors the flowers of the species. It was first registered with the Royal Horticultural Society in 1900. The green and white striping produces an intriguing color combination that makes it as popular today as when it was originated. It may be found in nearly all orchid collections. These *Paphiopedilums* are easy to grow into specimen plants, even on a windowsill or under lights, and a full pot may produce five or six flowers. As with other *Paphiopedilums*, the flowers may last for two months in perfect form. The plants require somewhat warmer growing conditions than the cool-growing Indian species with solid green leaves.

ORANGE CATTLEYA

CATTLEYA
C. aurantiaca

❧

This is a tolerant species found in Mexico and Central America. It is relatively common and tolerates exposure to sun and heat, desirable characteristics it passes on to its many hybrids today. In addition it is floriferous and contributes to the production of red, orange, and yellow flowers. It also hybridizes in nature with *Cattleya skinneri,* the national flower of Guatemala, to produce *C. guatemalensis,* which varies from red and orange to salmon and purple and even, rarely, to yellow and white. Certain Central American areas produce a type of self-pollinating flower that forms clusters of seedpods without even opening. Needless to say, these types are not as desirable horticulturally as the others. It is possible to grow fine specimen plants of *C. aurantiaca,* and a recent award-winner was about a meter across with hundreds of flowers in neat orange heads.

PALM-POLLY

POLYRADICION
P. lindenii

~

The Palm-Polly of Florida grows in the Everglades, a few feet above the water on treetrunks in the moist, shady, green environment. It has a few tropical relatives, and they are all unique in the orchid world in having no true leaves, only the fleshy green roots that carry out both absorption and food making for the plants. The flower stalks emerge from the crown of the plant, and the strikingly unique flowers are produced in the gloom, pollinated by night-flying insects.

PARISH'S VANDOPSIS

VANDOPSIS

V. parishii

~

Vandopsis is a genus from Burma and Thailand with strange spotted flowers that are fleshy green with a red lip. There also occurs a completely maroon-colored variety of the species with rounder-shaped flowers, all of the spots coalescing so that the darker color blocks out the green. Recently these flowers have been used to hybridize with *Vandas* and other Asian orchids to produce flowers with new forms and colors, especially reddish tones. The plants have very fleshy, hard, leathery leaves. This species was discovered in Moulmein in 1862 by the Reverend Parish and sent back to England for cultivation.

PHILIPPINE
PAPHIOPEDILUM

PAPHIOPEDILUM
P. philippinensis

~

A unique species and an instant favorite, with its boldly striped sepals and its long, twisted red-brown petals, this orchid came from the Philippines to England in 1864, where it was introduced to cultivation. This species usually flowers in June or July and enjoys the heat and humidity near the Equator, where it can grow in nearly full sun on limestone cliffs and boulders. In cultivation it definitely requires more light and heat than its close relatives. It was collected on the island of Guimares by John Gould, who had been searching for another orchid. When he found that orchid, this one was growing among its roots. It is popular today as a parent in producing unusual hybrids with the "Fu Manchu" petals.

PINK PHALAENOPSIS
HYBRID

PHALAENOPSIS
P. violacea x James McPherson

~

Phalaenopsis violacea hybrids are very sweetly fragrant. The leaves of this cross are characteristically broad and shiny and have a typically wavy margin. The flowers are heavy-textured, and the red-purple color is most pleasing, especially as it is set off by the thin white rim around the petals. Again characteristic of *P. violacea*, a parent that dominates in this hybrid, the flowers are not in the usual long sprays characteristic of other pink or white phalaenopsis. The James McPherson parent is a white *Phalaenopsis* with pink-striped petals and a deep red lip. It seems to have had little influence on the shape or coloration of this flower, though with further breeding its genes may show some domination for completely new patterns or colors.

PORPHYRIN-LIPPED

CATTLEYA

CATTLEYA
C. porphyroglossa

❦

This is an uncommon bifoliate *Cattleya* from Brazil, though the specimen illustrated has three leaves, as indeed several of the bifoliate species do from time to time. It has a very limited distribution, at least today—only for a short distance along one or two rivers, on low trees in swamps and on a few islands. It was thought extinct until a few plants were refound, and now it is being grown from seed in cultivation. It is not particularly attractive, with flowers small in proportion to the plant size and of a dull olive-brown coloration. The name means that the lip is colored porphyrin purple, and that color is produced by the colored raised granules that occur on a creamy background. The lateral lobes of the lip are white outside and inside are purple-veined with a light yellow to pink background. Originally considered to be a variety of another species, this orchid is now recognized as a separate one. It is sweetly scented.

PRIDE OF
TABLE MOUNTAIN

DISA

D. uniflora

~

Also called the Red Disa, this is one of about seventy
species of *Disa* endemic in South Africa. The Red
Disa may be found growing on Table Mountain, and
other species in the alpine grassland of the
Drakensberg. It has been featured on South African
stamps and in the logo of the Tenth World Orchid
Conference, held in Durban in 1981. This *Disa*
grows in moist or wet situations beside fresh water
and requires cool growing conditions of 40° to 60°
F. Although it is hard to handle in cultivation, some
growers have mastered the job and have not only
raised it from seed but have also produced a few
hybrids with other species.

PRIMROSE DENDROBIUM

DENDROBIUM
D. primulinum

~

Dendrobium is one of the largest genera throughout tropical Asia, Australia, and the South Pacific islands, particularly Papua New Guinea, with hundreds of species. Some of the showiest, with brightly colored hanging flowers, are from the hills of northern India. Some individual flowers of some species can last as long as six months (another orchid record!) and others may last only a few hours, less than a day. Many, like this species, are seasonal growers, growing in the wet, warmer time of year and losing their leaves completely to flower from the bare stems in the drier, cooler season. Altogether a remarkable group of species taking advantage of every ecological niche! The general appearance and fragrance of the flowers must have reminded the discoverer of primroses.

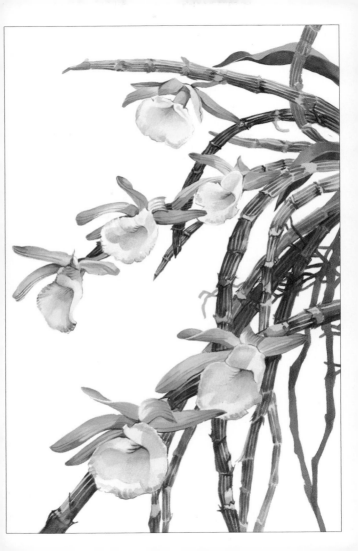

RED-SPECKLED LYCASTE

LYCASTE
L. cruenta

~

There are a number of similar yellow *Lycaste* species, all of which lose their leaves in the winter and flower along with their renewal of growth in the spring. With one or two exceptions, they are found in Central America. This one, with its sweet fragrance, is among the most common. A small plant can produce a whole wreath of flowers encircling the pot. They are popular among hobbyists because they are easy to grow, and their large pleated leaves have a lush tropical appearance. It is necessary to keep the plants quite dry during the winter to observe their dormancy period. The hallmark of yellow *Lycastes* is the presence of two sharp spines at the apex of the pseudobulb, which appear when the leaf turns yellow and falls. The name *cruenta* means "blood-stained" and refers to the red speckles and markings on the lip. This species has been in cultivation in England since 1842.

RICHARD MUELLER

BRASSOLAELIA

Brassavola nodosa x *Laelia milleri*, 1965

~

Brassavola nodosa is an excellent parent of many primary hybrids because its white flowers are dominant for shape but pick up the coloration and markings of the other parent. In this case the other parent is an orange-red *Laelia milleri* from Brazil. The speckles are always present in the hybrids, a contribution from the *nodosa*. Plants like sunny situations and well-drained potting mixes and are a good sort for beginners to grow. The leaves are fleshy and rounded and the plants compact. Some people like them so much they collect only *nodosa* hybrids.

Rosy-columneD
Aerangis

Aerangis
A. luteoalba var. *rhodosticta*

~

This orchid is tricky to grow, but the pretty white flowers with red columns make it an instant favorite. It comes from Kenya, Uganda, the Congo, and nearby areas and grows on forest trees in warm, moist locations near rivers or waterfalls. A fine specimen can be grown, with multiple sprays, and the plants always do best when mounted on a branch or slab of cork so the roots can be exposed. *Aerangis* is an African-Malagasian genus with more than seventy species; almost all have white flowers with nectar spurs hanging from the lips. Most are pollinated by moths with long tongues that can reach the nectar.

SANGUINE BROUGHTONIA

BROUGHTONIA
B. sanguinea

~

A species endemic to Jamaica, this *Broughtonia*
varies in color from a deep blood red (after which it
is named) to lighter shades of rosy purple. More
recently all-yellow and all-white forms have been
discovered, and they are very much in demand. The
plants require much humidity and sun and are
tough and leathery with long roots attached to the
tree trunks or fence posts where they may grow in
nature. The plants observe a definite winter
dormancy when they should not be watered very
much in cultivation. In summer the flower stalk may
rebranch, extending the blooming season to nearly a
year. A fine specimen clump can produce several
stalks and form a whole sunburst of bloom. The
bright rounded, flat flowers are popular in modern
hybridizing with *Cattleyas,* which usually produces
miniature red-flowering plants. They can be real
spotlights of color and are always at a premium. The
genus is named after Arthur Broughton, an English
botanist, and was introduced at Kew in 1793.

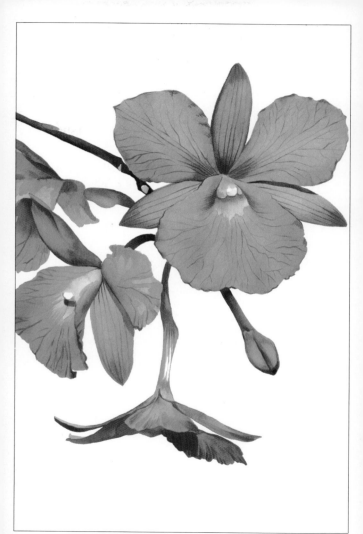

SCARLET SOPHRONITIS

SOPHRONTIS
Sophronitis coccinea (grandiflora)

～

A native to the cloud-shrouded forests of coastal Brazil, this *Sophronitis* is used for breeding modern red hybrids of miniature plant size. In nature, these flowers shine like spotlights in the forests, and make equally showy specimens in the cool, moist greenhouse. Some Japanese orchid growers specialize in this species alone, and may have as many as 500 specimens, or more, in a small greenhouse.

SPARKES' CYMBIDIUM

CYMBIDIUM

C. canaliculatum var. *sparkesii*

～

Another inhabitant of warm, or even hot, areas, and dry besides, this orchid is found in northern Australia and down into inland regions of eastern Queensland to New South Wales. The plants grow on trees and have tough, leathery, upright leaves. The sprays of flowers hang down below the leaves. Flowers vary in color from clear green, the so-called *alba* variety, to spotted, to a solid, deep red-brown in variety *sparkesii*. In fact, from a distance, the flowers can appear black, but they are not. (Black flowers don't really exist, except in myth and the literary imagination, or the popular "Brenda Starr" comic strip. They are very dark purple or red, usually with a velvety surface that doesn't reflect light—thus causing the illusion.) The plants are not easy to grow in cultivation, but the display is well worth it when they do well.

SPOTTED ONCIDIUM

ONCIDIUM
O. maculatum

This species grows from central Mexico south through Guatemala and neighboring countries. It is very variable in the size and number of flowers, but not in color. One form has been found, though, that completely lacks the spottings. Various forms are used today in breeding new *Oncidium* hybrids, and one of the most successful is called *Odontocidium* Big Mac—indeed it appears as a larger version of the species but is a little more yellow where this one is green. The shape and spotting of the flowers are genetically dominant in such hybrids. In nature, the species is fairly common in mountain areas, and the cream-colored lip may be undivided or have as many as five lobes.

SUMATRA MOTH ORCHID

PHALAENOPSIS

P. sumatrana

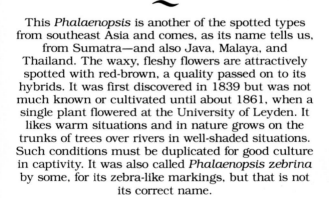

This *Phalaenopsis* is another of the spotted types
from southeast Asia and comes, as its name tells us,
from Sumatra—and also Java, Malaya, and
Thailand. The waxy, fleshy flowers are attractively
spotted with red-brown, a quality passed on to its
hybrids. It was first discovered in 1839 but was not
much known or cultivated until about 1861, when a
single plant flowered at the University of Leyden. It
likes warm situations and in nature grows on the
trunks of trees over rivers in well-shaded situations.
Such conditions must be duplicated for good culture
in captivity. It was also called *Phalaenopsis zebrina*
by some, for its zebra-like markings, but that is not
its correct name.

SWARTZ'S POLYSTACHYA

POLYSTACHYA
P. paniculata

~

Polystachya is an interesting genus with many species found in Africa, its center of origin. Only a few grow in South America and the Caribbean, and it is presumed their present distribution came about as a result of continental drift, when what is now South America split off from Africa to produce present-day geography. This particularly outstanding *Polystachya* has more flowers than most, and although they are individually small, the large panicle of burnt orange and tan makes them very showy. If you could look closely at each flower, you would see that the lip is on top, instead of turned around toward the bottom of the flower as in most orchids. This species was first described in 1799 by Swartz, who had collected some in Sierra Leone. The plants also grow in Zaire and Uganda.

TAMPA ENCYCLIA

ENCYCLIA

E. tampensis

～

The Tampa *Encyclia*, or Florida Butterfly Orchid
(though pollinated by small bees), was first found by
Dr. John Torrey in 1846 in early botanical
explorations of Florida. It is also rarely found in the
Bahamas. The plants usually grow on cypress trees
and will tolerate a certain amount of cold. It is now
protected by law, as are other Florida orchids (a
practice followed for orchids in other states as well),
and can be seen by the careful observer in many
parks and roadside stops. A number of cultivated
hybrids have been made, crossing it with *Cattleyas*
or other related types, and this produces plants with
graceful sprays of medium-sized flowers. The rare
green and white form, without the usual purple
markings, is especially desired.

TULIP ENCYCLIA

ENCYCLIA
E. citrina

~

This distinctive species has been classified as an *Epidendrum*, a *Cattleya*, and an *Encyclia*. In all correctness it deserves its own separate genus as it is not like anything else. The plants are found in the mountains of southern Mexico near Oaxaca, and the gray-green foliage always grows hanging down from the bottom of tree branches. The waxy flowers are usually single; rarely there are two or three. They are extremely fragrant, with a scent like orange blossoms, and last several weeks. This orchid has always attracted attention and was first described by the Jesuit Francisco Hernández who wrote on Mexican natural history in the seventeenth century. The Aztec name for this plant was *corticoatzontecoxochitl*. We can be grateful to call it simply *Encyclia citrina*.

WAXY RHYNCHOLAELIA

RHYNCHOLAELIA
(Brassavola) glauca

~

Native to Guatemala and other neighboring countries
of Central America, this orchid is noted for its tough,
leathery leaves and its slow, deliberate growth. The
plants must be well established to bloom, but their
white and green waxiness makes the flowers worth
waiting for. The large single flowers are sweetly
fragrant. The plants tolerate heat and light and grow
in comparatively low humidity. The species flowers
in February and March and has been used in several
hybrids because of its appealing shape and texture.

WHIDBEY ISLAND

BAKERARA
Aliceara Pacesetter x *Odontoglossum* Gold Basin, 1978

Some of these flowers are missing some of the standard orchid parts, and in others they are fused together in abnormal fashion. That is not unknown in complex hybrids such as *Bakeraras*, and it shows a certain lack of harmony in combining the various genera. The advantage of doing so, however, is that certain plants can be more easily grown than their parents. They no longer require such cool, humid growing conditions. Such is the case here. In complex hybrids with a combination of three or more genera—and this one has four *(Brassia, Oncidium, Odontoglossum, Miltonia)*—a new name is created for the genus by adding *ara* to a person's name—someone the originator wishes to commemorate.

WINGED ENCYCLIA

ENCYCLIA
E. alata

~

A typical pseudobulbous-stemmed *Epidendrum*
type, this Winged *Encyclia* was found by G. Ure
Skinner in 1837 in Honduras. Afterward it was
found in Mexico and other Central American
countries. The flowers are sweetly fragrant and vary
in color from an olive green to nearly brown. The
orangy yellow ruffle on the front edge of the lip and
the clear yellow lateral lobes are its hallmarks.
Hybridizers are gradually realizing that it makes a
good parent with *Cattleyas* or *Laelias*, as the large
flowers, ruffled lip, and the red veinings are all
desirable qualities. In addition, it is easy to grow and
flowers freely. In all ways, a good plant to have
around!

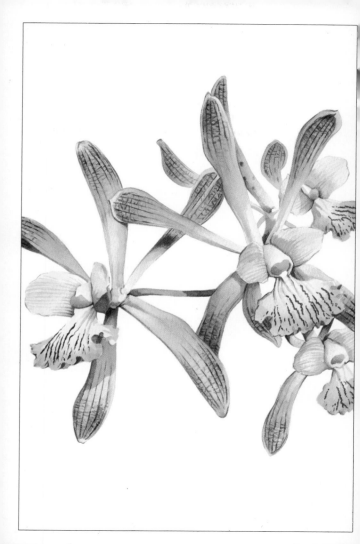

WOLTER'S
PAPHIOPEDILUM

PAPHIOPEDILUM
P. wolterianum

~

The tall, straight stems of Wolter's *Paphiopedilum* are distinctive and a characteristic much desired. (Many *Paphiopedilums* have short stems that almost hide the flowers among the leaves.) The slipper-like lips also show well in this illustration, as well as the green staminode, which is a developmentally sterile stamen that no longer produces pollen. The lady's slippers are among the most primitive of orchids, evolutionarily speaking, and have two functional stamens in contrast to most other orchids, which have only one. The loss of parts is one botanical way in which flower parts become specialized, and the orchids excel in their remarkable adaptation to insect pollinators. Today the proper name for this species is *Paphiopedilum appletonianum,* but it is still often known by its incorrect name. The species comes from Assam, in India, and Thailand.

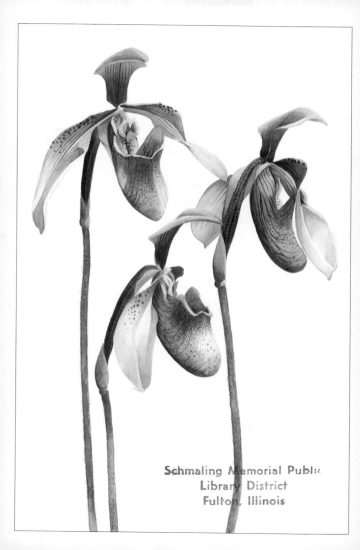

ORCHID CULTIVATION

It has been said, "If you can grow ferns, begonias, or African violets, you can grow orchids." In many ways this is true. These plants all require, within narrow limits, specific light conditions and a relatively high humidity for successful culture. Two points often overlooked, though, are getting to know what kinds of orchids are available and choosing plants that will flourish under the conditions that *you* can provide.

You will want to talk with other orchid growers, perhaps join a local society to see their show-table, and, most important, read some of the great numbers of available books and magazines that highlight orchid cultivation. Many times at orchid shows or society meetings beginners' plants are available for sale at reasonable prices. It is good to start out with three or four mature plants of various kinds. Find out by trial and error which will flower best for you. Growing orchids requires patience and experience, but with a few plants you should have at least one that will always be "doing" something—new lead growths of shoots or roots, leaves developing, flower stalks arising, blooms opening. Some orchids have dormant periods when only the status quo is apparent and no new growth or development is occurring. When you've gained some experience with mature plants, you can begin to experiment with growing seedlings. You should expect that it will take from one to two years for new plants to adapt to their surroundings and really come along; this depends, of course, on how "green" your thumb may be.

Orchids have the same basic growth requirements as do all plants, but the appropriate combination of these factors is often more critical for orchid cultivation than for other plants. These factors include proper temperature, good light, adequate humidity, continued air circulation, suitable potting material, methodical watering, balanced fertilizing, and freedom from pests and diseases. The supply of good light and sufficient humidity are often the most critical elements in home orchid growing.

Three temperature categories for orchids are recognized: cool (50°–55°F.), intermediate (about 60°F.), and warm (65°–70°F.). This refers to nighttime temperatures. A 10 to 15 degree differential between night and day is a necessity for successful orchid culture. Intermediate orchids match our own living requirements well, though a cool windowsill or northern exposure can be used for the cool types. Try any of the following, as they are good beginners' plants that can grow and flower under either cool or intermediate conditions: *Brassavola nodosa, Cattleya aurantiaca, Epidendrum cochleatum, Dendrobium nobile, Paphiopedilum villosum, Oncidium sphacelatum* or *Oncidium maculatum*. Warm growers, such as *Phalaenopsis* species or hybrids, or the spotted-leaved lady slippers are especially good for culture under lights or in a warm, south-facing room. A large standard or a small miniature cymbidium will do well on a well-lighted, cool sunporch or bay window. Sometimes moving the plant from one window to another will make a difference until you discover the combination the plant likes best.

Light is sometimes more important than temperature, and light often controls the other variables that affect whether your plant flowers or not. Most orchids enjoy good light and prefer growing in a southern or eastern exposure, sometimes directly in the sun. Morning light is preferred over the hotter noon and afternoon beams that can dehydrate the plants. If the leaves turn yellow, the plants may be receiving too much light and their growth will be stunted. If the plant growths are soft and floppy, too dark a green, and without flowers, the orchid is probably not getting enough light. If each new growth is larger than the previous one, and, once mature in size, a number of flowers are produced, then you've given your orchid proper care.

Humidity, as distinct from watering, should fall between

50 percent and 60 percent—or even 70 percent—so misting the plants at midday or midafternoon is often desirable. Or, have them growing with other plants or with a humidifier. It will make the air more comfortable for you too, especially if you have hot-air heat. The results of sufficient humidity will provide well-expanded leaves and pseudobulbs, well-opened flowers, and aerial roots that continue their growth over the edge of the flowerpot.

You should take care when you water the plants, drenching the potting material once or twice a week; dormant orchids or those with tough pseudobulbous stems and leaves need watering less often than the others. Just be certain that the plants have dried off by evening when the temperature goes down—no liquid drops should remain on or at the leaf angles where a rot could begin. A little fertilizer added to the water, about one-quarter the amount specified, is desirable; you can increase the amount a little when very active growth occurs.

Plastic pots are used often today, but some growers still prefer to use clay pots, though the clay pots—especially if small—dry out more quickly. The clay containers are often placed on racks over pans of wet gravel to increase the humidity. Orchids need repotting every two or three years into new mix—whatever kind you may find available: coarse, peaty compost; mixtures of bark, coarse pumice granules, and charcoal; crushed lava rock; coarse fern roots of various sorts; or sometimes sphagnum moss—just no soil. The mixtures must be long-lasting, porous, and well-drained so the orchid roots with their velamen layers receive plenty of air. Remember you are, most of the time, trying to duplicate conditions on a tree trunk in the tropics.

Finally, don't be intimidated or afraid to experiment! Orchids grow slowly and they die slowly. If things don't seem right, change the conditions. All growers—even the experts—have killed a few plants in their time. When your first flowers come along, you'll be more than pleased! And then you'll want another plant—and another.

GLOSSARY

AERIAL ROOT
A root that hangs from the stem into the air unattached to a support. Common on many epiphytes and climbers in the tropics.

CALYX
A collective term for all the sepals of a flower.

CANE-TYPE
Having a coarse upright stem that is strong but still fleshy and looking like a short section of sugar cane or similar plant.

CARPEL
The female organ of a flower, a unit or section of the fruit or pod that bears seeds inside. There are three carpels in orchid fruits.

CLONING
Reproducing the same plant repeatedly by vegetative techniques with cuttings, budding, grafting, divisions, etc., or by microscopic tissue culturing or meristemming techniques in the laboratory.

COLUMN
The fused tissue combining both stamens and pistils, or their modifications, in the center of the flower.

COOL-GROWING
Requiring night temperatures around 50° to 55°F. and a moderate daytime environment.

CROSS
Mating two different parents to produce a new population.

CULTIVAR

A single plant selected from a species or hybrid population because of distinguishing quality of form or color; the same as the older term, *variety*, when used horticulturally.

EPIPHYTE

A plant that is growing upon another plant and that is physically supported by it but *not* parasitizing the host plant.

GENUS

A collection of closely related species in a given family of plants or animals.

INTERSECTIONAL

Hybrid made between species or hybrids representing two sometimes widely different species classified in different subgenera of a large genus.

LEAD

The new growth from the main dormant bud at the base of the preceding growth.

LIP (LABELLUM)

The special petal of the orchid flower that serves to help attract the pollinator. It is usually positioned and formed to be a "landing platform" and aid in the pollination process.

MERISTEMMING

A laboratory process employed to reproduce especially fine plants, usually genetically identical, by culturing the growing point (meristem) tissue from the stem tip of a given plant.

MULTIGENERIC

Referring to a hybrid plant with parents that are also hybrids, usually of different sorts, so that the offspring represent a combination of up to six genera in one.

MYCORRHIZA
The combination of a root and a beneficial soil fungus that grows on decaying organic matter, helping the root to absorb nutrients and providing certain organic compounds, especially sugars, vitamins, and amino acids produced by the fungal metabolism.

POLYPLOID
Having more than the usual two sets of chromosomes in the nucleus of each cell, usually three or four (triploid, tetraploid), but sometimes more.

PRIMARY CROSS
A hybrid produced by mating two different species (*see also* Multigeneric).

PSEUDOBULB
A usually spherical or pear-shaped, fleshy, hard stem of many orchids; a stem adapted for water storage.

REED-STEMMED
Having a tall, usually stiff and strong, stem that is only a few millimeters in diameter—as contrasted with cane-stemmed or pseudobulbous orchids.

SEPAL, DORSAL
Three sepals compose the calyx of a flower. This sepal is located opposite the lip petal and is usually the uppermost part of epiphytic orchid flowers.

SPUR
A nectar-containing tubelike extension from the base of the lip petal. It can be short and wide or long and narrow.

STAMEN
A male element that bears pollen grains in the flower.

TISSUE CULTURE
The growing of plant tissues in test tubes on sterile nutrient medium and the propagation of new plants from such tissue.

VARIETY
An older horticultural designation for a plant distinguished in its population by fine color or form and usually given a name, in single quotation marks, for marking that distinction (*see also* Cultivar).

VELAMEN
A spongy multilayered epidermis on orchid roots that can temporarily absorb water or dissolved nutrients, passing them on into the root. The velamen can also attach the root to the tree or other substrate.

ABOUT THE AUTHOR

Dr. Carl Withner's involvement with the horticultural world extends back over forty years. He holds a Ph.D. in plant physiology from Yale University and is a retired Professor Emeritus of biology from Brooklyn College in New York. He acted as curator of the orchid collection at the Brooklyn Botanic Garden for three decades and is an accredited judge of the American Orchid Society. Dr. Withner has judged shows internationally in places as diverse as Australia, Singapore, Italy, Switzerland, and South America. Among his published credits are *The Orchids: A Scientific Study* (John Wiley & Sons), *An Encyclopedia of Roses* (Prentice-Hall), and over one thousand articles in horticultural journals, including the *Orchid Review* published by the Royal Horticultural Society.